*To my daughter Lily,
this book is for you.
I love you more than
all the stars in the sky.*

Copyright © 2020 Nattie Kate Mason
ISBN Print: 978 0648485 360
All rights reserved. No part of this publication may be reproduced, stored in or introduced into a retrieval system, or transmitted in any form or by any means without the prior written permission of the author and publisher.
Cover and interior illustrator: Jasmine Berry
Copy editor: Chelsea Taylor
Series: The Adventure of Lily Rose
Series book number: 1

LILY ROSE AND THE PEARL CROWN

Nattie Kate

LILY ROSE TURNS 9!

Hi! My name is LILY ROSE GARDINER and today is the best day of the year! Do you know why? It's because today is my 9th BIRTHDAY!!!

My sister and I go to Willows Beach Primary School and this year I am in year four. My teacher Miss Sandford is really nice, but sometimes she can be a teeny tiny bit strict. Chloe, my younger sister, is seven years old and she is in Mrs. Mason's year three class.

Chloe and I live with our mum, dad, snobby cat DUTCHIE and gentle giant dog JACK in the small beach town of Willow's

Bay. Our LAVENDER painted cottage is the prettiest house on the street, and we have our own special tree house in the front yard.

From our fort we can SPY all the way to the OCEAN! Our treehouse is the best treehouse ever! It has comfy beanbags, a tea set, lots of toys, spy gear and mountains of books inside.

Mum and dad don't have much of a green thumb, that means they aren't very good at keeping plants alive. Mum says that's why we don't have many flowers in our garden.

My mum **LOVES** plants, sadly they just don't seem to love her back. If the plants look healthy, mum waters them. If she's already watered them, she'll water them again to make sure they get a good drink. If a plant looks like a dead twiggy stick, mum will still water it.

Mum waters her plants so much that I think they must die from too much love. But the flowers and plants that do grow are very pretty.

Anyway, back to me! I *LOVE* to do *GYMNASTICS, ART, DANCE* and *SING*. I can do so many tricks I bet I could join the circus!

I may not be the top of my class at school, but mum tells me that I have something special that sadly lots of kids these days don't have. I have an amazing IMAGINATION.

But do you want to know a secret? My favourite thing to do is READ!!!

Life is never dull when you have a good book and an imagination. At least that's what my mum always says.

I have been on so many amazing adventures through reading books. But I hope I get to go on a real adventure one day. Wouldn't it be amazing to sail on a PIRATE SHIP and search for real buried treasure? Or imagine swimming with MERMAIDS in the sea or flying on a BROOMSTICK at MAGIC SCHOOL!!!

If I had magical powers, I would turn the boys at school into TOADS and race them for fun! The winner would get to be turned back into a real boy and the losers would become our new CLASS PETS.

Since today is my birthday, we are going to have a picnic at the beach with my best friend Lilsie. Her real name is Lily too, but we all call her Lilsie, so we don't get mixed up. When we

play together, mum calls us
DOUBLE TROUBLE!

Lilsie and I have been BFFS since preschool. She has bright blue eyes just like me, but her brown hair is SUPER CURLY. My brown hair is a little bit shorter now because my mum made me have a haircut. I hate haircuts! But mum says my hair will grow back longer and healthier now. I hope she's right because I want it to grow so long that I can SWING ON IT just like Rapunzel.

"Lily Rose! Breakfast's ready!" mum called from the kitchen.

YUM! I wonder what could be for breakfast. Maybe it's blueberry pancakes or bacon and eggs. Maybe she shaped the pancakes into heart or star shapes and sprinkled chocolate sauce all over them. That would be DELICIOUS!

"Coming mum!" I called, as I made my way to the dining room.

Chloe and dad were already digging into breakfast when I got to the table.

"HAPPY BIRTHDAY!!!" they shout.

"Thanks!"

I have the biggest smile across my face because on my plate is a massive stack of PINK HEART shaped pancakes!

"YUM! Thanks mum! These look great!" I exclaimed.

"Don't look at the bottoms," mum warned. "They might be a little burnt. I got distracted making tea, sorry."

Did I mention mum's a really bad cook? She tries hard but cooking just isn't her thing.

DAD has always been the **BEST COOK** in the family, but I'm catching up to him. I can cook eggs on toast already. Don't tell mum, but Dad says I'm a better cook than her.

I decide to take mum's advice and not check the underside of the pancakes. I covered my pancakes with strawberries and maple syrup. When I took a bite, I could hardly even taste the burnt bits.

It's Sunday today, so we don't have to rush off to school or work. After breakfast, we all head out to the lounge room to open my presents. Opening presents is one of the BEST things about birthdays.

"Here you go sweetie," mum says, passing me a large box wrapped in rainbow paper.

"Thanks mum!"

I give the box a **LITTLE SHAKE** and try to guess what's inside. It doesn't make any noise, so I give up and rip the wrapping open instead.

Inside the box is a super cute **TEDDY**. It looks really old but, it's wearing a fancy new **MERMAID** outfit. I **LOVE** it!

"Thanks mum!"
"Her name is Teddy," mum tells me. "Teddy was given to me

when I was your age. I thought you might like to take care of her now."

"Thanks mum! I love her!" I say, giving Teddy a test cuddle.

Teddy smells just like mum, like *TEA* and *FLOWERS*.

Chloe is squirming around beside me eager to give me her present. She shoves a rectangular box on my lap. It is wrapped in homemade paper with pretty pictures of blue mermaids and blue seashells.

Chloe draws everything in blue because blue is her favourite colour. All her toys and clothes are blue. Even her quilt cover is blue. EVERYTHING IS BLUE. I hate blue.

"Hurry up and open it," she begs excitedly.
Chloe and I are almost the same height even though I'm a year older than her. I don't

know where I got my tall legs from. Mum and dad are both short, but I think I'll be taller than mum soon.

Chloe's eyes are brown, and she has the same wavy light brown hair that I do. But her hair is much longer than mine and is braided back beautifully with a blue ribbon on the end.

I open the present and inside is a BLUE book about the BLUE fairy.

"Thanks Chloe! It's beautiful," I say, but not because it is blue.

I really do not love the colour blue, but the book does look super pretty and I love books. I open it and realize it's also a POP-UP BOOK! Pop-up books are the coolest! Tiny intricate details of FLOWERS and FAIRIES in a MAGICAL GARDEN are cut out into the paper and it makes the book look like it has come to life.

"I love it!" I say putting the book aside to give my sister a big warm hug.

Chloe has a big smile upon her face. "I always give the best presents!" Chloe boasts proudly.

"My turn," Dad interrupts, passing me my last gift.
It is an old wooden chest about the size of a shoe box with

drawings of the ocean and MERMAIDS carved into it.

"Thanks dad," I say, carefully opening the wooden box.

Chloe and I gasp as we behold what's inside. I reach into the box and pull out a beautiful PEARL CROWN. The whole crown is made of shells of different shapes and sizes. Arranged beautifully amongst the shells are pink and white pearls. I have never seen anything like it before!

"Thank you so much dad! I LOVE it!" I squeal, admiring the crown.

"You're welcome Lil. I found it at a local antique shop and thought it would be perfect for when you and Chloe play dress-ups," he replied. "Teddy can even join in with her mermaid costume," he smiled at mum.

"Thanks dad! It looks like something straight out of a FAIRY TALE. I love it!"

I give mum and dad both a big squeezy bear hug. This is going to be the BEST BIRTHDAY.

PLAY TIME

Chloe and I spent the morning playing in our tree house. It is our favourite spot to play because it's just us kids, NO ADULTS allowed!

Today we are dressed up as mermaids and I am wearing my new pearl crown. Chloe wanted to wear it, but mum said since it's my birthday that I don't have to share it if I don't want to.

Can you guess what colour Chloe's mermaid outfit is? That's right, it's BLUE! Mine is PINK. Teddy is sitting beside me in her new mermaid outfit too. She looks super cute.

My sister and I have been pretending we are mermaid princesses having an under the sea tea party. We have chocolate cupcakes with sprinkles and lavender tea to share. Our teapot and teacups have pretty pictures of LILIES AND ROSES painted on them just like my name!

"Lily Rose! Chloe! Time to get ready for the picnic. Lilsie will be here any minute," mum calls from the bottom of the treehouse ladder.

"Coming mum!" we both call.

Mum made her way back inside while we quickly packed up our tea set.

"Teddy, I'm sorry but you better stay home today. I don't want you to get all sandy and wet at the beach," I tell her as I tuck Teddy up with a blanket on one of the beanbags.

Chloe has already made her way down the ladder. I take a quick look out at the beach from high up in our fort. The weather is perfect today!

As I looked out over the sparkling water, I spotted something SHIMMERING. It looked like a fin, but it was too big to be a fish. That's weird! As quick as it appeared, it is gone again. I wonder what it could have been. I think I'll have another look for it when I am down at the beach.

"See you later Teddy!" I call as I make my way down the rope ladder.

Just as I reach the ground a red car pulls up in the driveway. It's Lilsie! She jumps out of the car dressed in her own red mermaid costume, just as excited to see me as I am to see her.

"**LILSIE**!" I yell as I run to give her a big welcome hug.

"**HAPPY BIRTHDAY** Lily!" she replies, hugging me back extra tight before handing me a gift bag. "I made you a present! Open it up!"

I am so excited to see what she has given me that I sit on the grass and open it straight away.

"Happy Birthday Lily Rose! Bye Lilsie," her mum calls from the car. "I'll pick you up just before dinner," she says as she starts to reverse out of the driveway.

"Bye mum!" Lilsie calls.

Her mum waves goodbye as she drives away. I can't wait to spend the whole afternoon with my best friend. This is going to be the best day ever!

I turn back to the gift bag and pull out the tiny present

wrapped in gold tissue paper. As I open it, I realize it's a SEASHELL NECKLACE. Even better, it matches my new crown PERFECTLY!

"Thanks, Lilsie!" I squeal in delight as I slip it over my head.

"You're welcome!" she replies. "I wanted to make you something extra special for your birthday rather than buying you a present. I found this pretty shell at the beach and mum helped me turn it into a necklace. I hope you like it."

"I LOVE it!" I exclaim. "I can't wait to show it to my family. It goes beautifully with my mermaid costume. Thank you so much."

Lilsie and I skip arm in arm into the cottage to find mum, dad and Chloe. They are all busy in the kitchen packing the last of the party food into the picnic basket.

Mum has baked me a DELICIOUS birthday cake. I think it is meant to be a mermaid, but I'm not entirely sure. If you squint your eyes and look at it sideways it kind of looks like a mermaid's tail coming out of the ocean.

I'm sure it TASTES BETTER than it LOOKS. Mum's cakes always end up tasting amazing. It's one of the few things she's good at cooking. But don't tell mum I said that. Shh.... It'll be our little secret.

"Hello Lilsie!" mum greets my bff. "Ready to go girls? I'm just finishing packing now."

"We're ready," we giggled.

"Lily, can you please put Jack's leash on so we can leave?" Dad asks.

Jack is our **BIG** brown dog.

I call him my gentle giant because he is as big as a horse, but as a cuddly as a teddy bear. Jack's even scared of our grumpy cat Dutchie.

"Yes dad!" I say.

Lilsie and I head out the back to put Jack's lead on. Jack is always super excited to see his lead because it means he's going for a walk.

"Ready!" I yell out, as we walk back through the house with Jack.

"Thank you, girls. Now let's go," Mum declares.

I sling the bag of towels over my shoulder and we all make our way out to Willows Bay beach, behind our house. It's PARTY time!

THE BEACH PICNIC

The weather is nice and sunny today, not a cloud in the sky. A gentle breeze is fluttering in from the ocean helping to keep us cool. At the end of the beach there are sea caves to explore and rock pools full of tiny creatures to discover.

Who knows what MAGICAL TREASURES are waiting to be found?

Jack enjoyed galloping in and out of the waves as we walked. Every time he got wet though he would shake himself off near dad and then jump back into the water again. It was really funny to watch.

"Before you go and explore, you need to eat first girls," mum announced once we got to our picnic spot.

Mum unpacked fruit salad, lollies, chips, a cheese platter and sandwiches for us to share. I ate heaps of lollies and chips, but then dad suggested I have some REAL FOOD because you need lots of energy to play.

The cheese and fruit salad were super yummy. But I didn't have time to sit around and chit chat, I wanted to go swimming and explore.

"Let's turn your mum and dad into MERMAIDS and then make a GIANT sandcastle," Lilsie suggested after we were all finished eating.

"That's a great idea!" Chloe agreed.

Mum and dad DID NOT look impressed with that idea, but they went along with it anyway. Mum and dad are pretty cool parents.

I didn't want to bury mum and dad or make a sandcastle. I just wanted to go and explore. But I guess my adventure could wait a little longer. It was Lilsie's idea after all.

After we buried mum and dad in the sand, turning their legs

into mermaid's tails, we built the BIGGEST sandcastle you have ever seen. It even had turrets and a moat for the water to flow around it. But it was still missing something.

"I KNOW!" I exclaimed. "Let's split up and find shells to decorate the castle!"

"That's a great idea!" Lilsie shouted and Chloe agreed.

We each grabbed a sand bucket and walked in different directions searching for pretty shells. I headed straight for the rock pools of course!

On my way there I found a lovely PURPLE clam shell that was almost as big as my hand. I have never seen such a huge shell before.

The tide was low, so the rock pools were shallow and GREAT for exploring.

Tiny little crabs scuttled around and black shell sea snails with speckled white dots were stuck to the rocks. I spotted a MASSIVE STARFISH at the bottom of one of the pools. It was bright blue; Chloe would love it.

I jumped from one rock to the next, careful to keep my balance and stay dry while I was still in my costume. The moss on the rocks made it a bit slippery, but it was lots of fun.

I collected some seaweed in my sand bucket to add to the sandcastle and a little extra to throw at Chloe. SEAWEED WARS are so much fun!

As I approached the edge of the pools where the ocean meets the rock shelf, I looked out over the surrounding rocks and spotted the shimmering fin again. I skipped from one rock to the next trying hard not to fall in the water, as I tried to get a better look.

"Oh my gosh! Lilsie is never going to believe this!" I exclaimed.

I couldn't believe it! Perched on top of a rock jutting out of the ocean was a REAL MERMAID! Her long tail was turquoise, and her scales shimmered in the sunlight. She wore a matching coloured crown made of shells and sea glass atop her head. Her long curly strawberry blond hair trailed behind just like

Rapunzel. She was the most beautiful thing I had ever seen!

A REAL MERMAID!

Have you ever dreamed of meeting a real mermaid? Ever since I was four years old, I have drawn pictures in the sand to leave as messages for the mermaids. I like to go back to the beach the next day to see if they have replied with a drawing of their own.

I never thought I would actually get to see a MERMAID!

Sitting upon a rock, wringing her hands in worry, was a real live mermaid!

"Hello!" I called eagerly trying to get her attention.

The mermaid noticed me for the first time and swiftly dived under the water out of sight.

"You can come out!" I called, "I'm not going to hurt you. I promise!"

After a few minutes with no further sign of the mermaid I released a heavy sigh and turned to head back to my family.

"Hello," a quiet sing-song voice whispered from the edge of the water.

I turned back around to find the mermaid resting her arms on the rocks, her tail hidden beneath the water.

"Hi!" I exclaimed, and in all my excitement to walk over to her, I lost my balance and slipped over the edge into the waves.

The water was deeper than I thought. I tried to swim up to

the surface, but my mermaid tail costume got stuck on a rock. The mermaid must have realized I was in trouble because she dived under the water and helped me up to the surface.

Then the weirdest thing happened! My legs began to feel all WARM AND TINGLY. As I looked down for the source of the weird sensation, I realized my legs had transformed into a

MERMAID TAIL! WOAH!

How did that happen?

It was then that I noticed the crown was warm and pulsing on my head. Both my tail and crown were now the same warm temperature. Oh my goodness, I am going to be in so much trouble with mum and dad!

"I knew that was OUR CROWN!" The mermaid

squealed with excitement. "Where did you find it?"

"What do you mean your crown? It's my crown! I was given it today for my birthday. Did you give me a mermaid tail?" I asked confused.

"It was the crown!" The mermaid stated as if it was obvious. "That is our mermaid Queen Celeste's pearl crown! It has been missing for a long time. It was carried away in the waves during a cyclone when I was little."

"Uh oh! Does that mean I am going to be a mermaid FOREVER? Mum and dad are going to miss me so much if I don't get back to them soon," I worried.

The mermaid chuckled, "No silly!" Then she pulled herself up onto the rock shelf before helping to pull me up too.

As soon as my tail was out of the water it thankfully turned back into my legs.

"WOW! That's so cool!" I squealed.

"Magical more like it. I'm Sapphire, Princess of the mer-kingdom," she greeted me.

I can't believe it! She's a REAL PRINCESS! Lilsie will never believe this!

"I'm Lily Rose," I introduced myself excitedly.

"Pleased to meet you Lily Rose!" Princess Sapphire replied.

"I hope it's not rude to ask, but why are you here Princess?" I asked. "Do you come to the beach often?"

"This is my FIRST TIME at the seashore," Sapphire explained. "It's beautiful! But mermaids aren't allowed to be seen by humans. It's not safe, so we have to stay away," she said sadly.

"What brings you here today?" Lily asked curiously.

"My family and the mermaid kingdom are in trouble," Sapphire explained. "A wicked Sea Witch stole my father's trident and locked all my family in our underwater castle dungeon. I didn't get caught because I was out exploring when the Sea Witch attacked the castle. Since then I have been swimming around looking for someone to help me save my family."

WOW!

A MERMAID KINGDOM.

A magical TRIDENT.

An evil SEA WITCH!

It all sounds like a fairy tale!

"I'll help you Sapphire!" I offered excitedly. "This is the adventure I have been waiting for!"

"It's lovely of you to offer Lily, but it's TOO DANGEROUS for a little girl," Sapphire warned.

"PLEASE let me help you!" I begged. "I'll be careful."

Sapphire bit her lip nervously. "Okay Lily, but if you feel

unsafe you must promise me that you will swim home."

"I promise!"

UNDER THE SEA

With not a moment to spare, I slipped off my costume tail and jumped back into the ocean. My legs tingled before shifting into a shimmering pink and purple scaled mermaids' tail.

I'M A MERMAID!

This is every girl's dream!

Swimming under the sea was incredible. Not only could I swim super-fast with a flap of my tail, I could also see just as clearly as if I was on land. The magic must be helping with that too.

I did a summersault in the water to test out my new tail! Gymnastics is so much fun in the water!

This crown is INCREDIBLE!
BEST BIRTHDAY PRESENT EVER!

As we began our journey to the mermaid kingdom, dolphins weaved around us playfully, guiding our way. Giant turtles swum gracefully along the ocean's currents. Schools of fish in every colour of the rainbow swam past us without a care.

I can't wait to tell Lilsie and Chloe all about my under the sea adventure! I'm sure they would love to borrow my crown and swim like a mermaid.

The water grew darker the deeper we swam. A crater in the ocean floor led to a drop so deep you couldn't see the bottom. I was curious to explore the basin below, but Sapphire grabbed my arm, holding me back.

"IT ISN'T SAFE! The Sea Witch lives down there with her minions. We need to move on," she whispered her warning.

With that in mind, onwards we quietly swam over the fissure in the ocean floor, headed for the mermaid kingdom.

After swimming for what felt like hours, Sapphire slowed down her pace. I followed her lead. She took my hand gently and with the other she held a single finger to her lips to signal to remain quiet.

It had all been so exciting, swimming like a MERMAID and meeting a MERMAID PRINCESS. That was until I remembered why we were here.

My body started to shake with worry as Sapphire pulled me into a small sea cave to hide. I wasn't sure why we were hiding, but a moment later three SLIMY EELS swum past the entrance.

They looked like they were hunting for someone or something. After a few minutes, Sapphire led me back out of the cave.

"It's ok Lily Rose, they have gone now," Sapphire tried to reassure me. "They were some of the SEA WITCHES MINIONS. She has a large group of eels in her service. No doubt they helped her steal the trident and capture my family."

I shook my head in despair. "How can I possibly help?" I worried. "I'm only nine! I can't save a mermaid kingdom!"

Sapphire looked at me with kind eyes.

"Have courage Lily Rose. Believe in yourself, as I believe in you," she spoke gently. "We can turn around and I will escort you back home if you like. But I have faith in you Lily.

TOGETHER we can do this. TOGETHER we can SAVE MY FAMILY and my kingdom."

I felt a little braver after hearing Sapphire's words of encouragement. I took a deep breath to calm myself.

"How can I help?" I asked with newfound confidence.

Huddled behind a rock Sapphire laid out her brilliant idea.

THE MERMAID KINGDOM

Do you remember watching 'The Little Mermaid' movie and seeing the underwater castle for the first time? Do you remember how dazzling it looked? The real thing is so much BETTER!

We snuck into Sapphires' bedroom through the balcony. As soon as there was a break in the eel patrols, we quickly swam from the safety of the coral sea beds in through the balcony doors.

Sapphire and I now hid in the shadows of her bedroom, looking out over the

MERMAID KINGDOM.
The view was MAGICAL!

The castle was as tall as a skyscraper made entirely out of various coloured CORAL. The castle was literally alive. There were balconies off each of the suites and a tall tower reaching towards the water's surface.

GLOW WORMS kept in sea glass domes, made the city

SHINE. Tiny houses made of coral with transparent sea glass windows, surrounded the castle forming a cute little underwater city.

Sea creatures swam carefree around the water while mer-people were corralled by eels into the depths of the castle.

"They're taking them to the dungeons," Sapphire whispered.

I could hear the hisses of the eels and the cries of scared mermaid children clinging to their parents. What sort of a witch would want to lock away KIDS? The Sea Witch needs to be stopped just like the villains in fairy tales.

"Are you ready Lily Rose?" Sapphire asked.

I took a deep breath to shake off the last of my fear. "Ready!" I whispered.

"Ok," Sapphire spoke calmly, "Just like we planned."

I nodded, "Lead the way."

THE SEA WITCH

Sapphire and I weaved our way through the underwater castle. At each corner we checked that the halls and stairs were clear before swimming towards our next hiding spot.

It was strange to see so many staircases in the castle. After all, don't mermaids just swim wherever they want to go?

Anyway, now that we had reached the seabed floor of the castle, we waited by hiding behind a curtain. Our plan was to slip in amongst a group of mermaids being escorted to the dungeons.

It didn't take long before a large group of mermaids were rushed past us. Carefully avoiding the SLIMY, DISGUSTING EELS, we slipped out from behind the curtain and joined the group.

There were at least EIGHT REVOLTING EELS surrounding us and the other mermaids. The thought of their slimy bodies anywhere near me, made my mermaid scales shiver.

Down into the dungeon we swam keeping an eye out for the evil Sea Witch. The dungeon was unlike anything I have ever seen. Cell after cell was filled with mermaids trapped behind sharp coral bars electrified by the eels to stop anyone trying to escape. Butterflies swarmed around my belly as I started to feel anxious again.

What am I doing here? I'm just a girl! I'm not a hero.

It was then that a voice as old as time cackled from the far end of the dungeon, sending shivers down my back.

The Sea Witch was more terrifying than any villain in my books. Instead of a mermaid tail, her PURPLE OCTOPUS like TENTACLES streamed around her waiting to trap their next prey. I hope it's not me!

"Welcome to your new home **PEASANTS**!" The Sea Witch cackled. "If you do not agree to serve me, you will spend the rest of your days in these cells. I am your Queen now and you shall all obey me or **FACE MY WRATH**!"

I didn't know what to do. I'd forgotten the plan and somehow, I had **LOST** Sapphire amongst the group.

The eels ushered us closer to the Sea Witch who held THE KINGS TRIDENT tight in her hand. A SPIKEY CROWN made of sea glass was perched upon her head.

The Sea Witch appraised us each in turn, searching for who or what, I wasn't sure. Her fierce gaze rested on me and my heart started racing.

"You!" She shrieked at me with a wicked grin. "Come here," she beckoned with her **CLAWED** finger.

Oh, my goodness! I need to get out of here! I frantically looked around for a way to escape, but I couldn't see a way out.

The Sea Witch grew impatient and ordered me to her again. Hesitantly, I weaved my way through the other mermaids and made my way to where the Sea Witch stood menacingly.

"WHO ARE YOU?" she demanded.

"My name is Lily Rose, Your Highness. Please don't hurt me. I mean you no harm," I stammered, my voice shaking with worry.

"Ha!" The Sea Witch cackled, "Of course you are no threat to me! You are a nobody and I am a witch. What could you ever do to harm me?!"

The dungeon went spookily silent. Even the children now were quiet for fear that their cries would draw the evil witch's attention.

"GIVE ME THAT CROWN!" the Sea Witch ordered, pointing to the pearl crown atop my head. "I don't know how you got it, but it belongs to me now, so hand it over or else!"

I knew I couldn't give her the crown, or I would turn back into an ordinary girl and drown. So, I held my head high and tried to summon all the courage of the hero's I had read about in books.

"No!" I yelled. "It doesn't belong to you and you are not the mermaid Queen! LET THE MER-PEOPLE GO!"

The Sea Witch attempted to launch herself at me to make a

grab for the crown. But whilst her attention was solely on me, she failed to notice what was happening around her.

Sapphire DOVE from the side KNOCKING THE SEA WITCH into the ocean floor before wrangling the trident out of her hand. Sapphire quickly pulled herself upright while the Sea Witch was still trying to UNTANGLE HER TENTACLES on the floor.

The mermaid princess pointed her father's trident at the Sea Witch and declared:

"SURRENDER SEA WITCH! Without the trident you are nothing!"

The Sea Witch released a frightening cackle as she finally righted herself.

"I am a Sea Witch! I don't need the trident to rule you all. I have magic of my own!" she bellowed.

But before she could cast a spell or make a move against Sapphire, I felt my Pearl Crown heat up and glow. The Queen's pearl crown released a powerful shot of white light at the enemy Witch, turning her into a TINY SEA SNAIL with a black shell and white spots.

Applause filled the dungeon as the Sea Witch was defeated. The people were protected by the crown that rightfully belonged to their Queen.

I still don't quite know how it happened. One second I was picturing turning the evil Witch into a snail and the next second she was. It was magic! Together, Sapphire and I had saved the Kingdom.

"THREE CHEERS FOR LILY ROSE!" Sapphire cheered.

As the mer-people applauded. I gave Sapphire a big squeezy hug. With the Sea Witch defeated, the eels quickly slithered away. No doubt to slink back to their home in the deep crack in the ocean floor.

THE END OF AN ADVENTURE

A special under the sea party was held to thank Sapphire and myself for saving the mermaid kingdom. The King's NEW PET sea snail 'WITCHY POO,' was stuck in her new bowl beside the King's throne. There he could keep a close eye on her in case she ever figured out how to turn herself back into a witch. But the King assured me that was very unlikely now that he had his trident back.

The MERMAID QUEEN was very happy to see her crown again and I promised that she could have it back as soon as I was safely back at the beach.

Sapphire agreed to deliver it back to the Queen for me. Sadly, that meant I'd never be able to transform into a mermaid again, but Sapphire promised to visit me at the beach so that was some good news.

After we had finished feasting on kelp cakes and seaweed juice, we danced under the light of the glow worms. But sadly, now it was time to swim home.

The mer-people formed two horizontal lines and created an archway for Sapphire and I to swim down in farewell and thanks. It was such a special moment. I will never forget this MAGICAL UNDER THE SEA KINGDOM.

It was a sad journey home. It's hard knowing that I will never see the mermaid kingdom again. But I am so very glad to have a MERMAID FRIEND of my very own. I wonder if Sapphire would like to meet Lilsie and Chloe? They would enjoy that very much.

Arriving where the rock pools meet the ocean, Sapphire helped me shimmy back onto the rock jutting out from the land, and she perched up beside me. As soon as my tail was out of the water the magic faded and my legs returned. I am going to miss my beautiful

PURPLE and PINK SHIMMERING TAIL.

I took the crown off my head and sadly gave it to Sapphire. The mermaid Princess replaced her own crown with the Queen's crown. Then to my surprise, she handed her own crown to me as a gift.

"This crown isn't magical, but I want you to have it. I hope that when you wear it, you will think of me and my home," Sapphire explained.

"Thank you so much! I will treasure this FOREVER!" I exclaimed, giving her a big hug.

Sapphire hugged me back and then slid gracefully back into the water. "Happy Birthday Lily Rose, I'll see you again soon," Sapphire promised.

"Goodbye Sapphire, I'll miss you!" I replied.

Then Sapphire, my friend, the mermaid princess dived back beneath the ocean's surface and began her journey back home. All the way to the magical under the sea kingdom.

SQUEEZY CUDDLES

"Lily Rose! Where are you?" I heard mum call as she approached the rock pools.

"Over here mum!" I yelled back making my way over to her.

Mum threw her arms around me and gave me the biggest SQUEEZY CUDDLE. Mum always gives the best hugs. "We have been so worried about you darling!" Mum stressed. "Where have you been? I have searched everywhere, but I couldn't find you."

"I'm ok mum! I just had an adventure that's all," I reassured her. A magical under the sea adventure I cheekily thought to myself.

"I am glad you're safe my little blossom. But next time could you adventure somewhere where we can see you please?" mum requested.

"Yes mum," I promised.

Mum sighed with relief, giving me another squeezy cuddle. "Let's go home. I think it's time for a nice HOT CHOCOLATE, and a MOVIE. Don't you?"

"Yesss! Can I pick the movie please? Chloe always gets to choose!"

"Absolutely!" Mum laughed. "It is your birthday after all."

Exploring under the sea was unforgettable, but as Dorothy says, there's no place like home.

About the Author:

Nattie Kate is an Aussie Author based in Perth. She lives with her hubby and daughter Lily, their gentle giant dog Jack and snobby cat Dutchie. Like the mum in 'The Adventures of Lily Rose' series, Nattie loves plants, but sadly they just don't love her back. Nattie began her writing journey publishing a young adult series called 'The Crowning'. She designed this chapter book series to be a bridge between early readers and middle grade books, targeted at clever younger readers who want a reading challenge.

Other titles in the Adventures of Lily Rose, Chapter Book series:
Lily Rose and the Enchanted Fairy Garden
(publication date: July 2020)
Lily Rose and the search for the Lost Treasure
(publication date: Aug 2020)
Lily Rose and the Magical Mirror
(Publication date: Sep 2020)

Young Adult fantasy titles by Nattie Kate Mason:
The Crowning
A Queen's Fate
Heart of a Crown

Website: nattiekatemason.com
Middle Grade Author page:
Instagram: @nattie.kate
Facebook: @nattie.kate.author
Young Adult Author page, Instagram and Facebook: @nattie.kate.mason.writer

www.ingramcontent.com/pod-product-compliance
Lightning Source LLC
Chambersburg PA
CBHW070309010526
44107CB00056B/2536